# TH__ __G

# 40

## FUNKY *and* 40

# THE BIG 40

## Your Survival Guide

An exclusive edition for

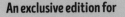

for all your gift books and gift stationery

This edition first published in Great Britain in 2018 by
Allsorted Ltd, Watford, Herts, UK WD19 4BG

© Susanna Geoghegan Gift Publishing

Author: Emma Hill

Cover design: Milestone Creative

ISBN: 978-1-911517-49-8

Printed in China

# THE BIG 40 IS UPON YOU!

What to do with the next decade of your life?
Firstly, you could dip into this book filled with
witticisms, truths, jokes and advice on turning
40. Sure, we can look back on your 20s and 30s
with wistful nostalgia; those heady days when a
hangover could be cured merely by the imbibing of
a full English and a vat of coffee, but mostly we're
looking ahead with optimism and enthusiasm,
comfortable in our own skin, definitely wiser and
ready to embark on a mid-life adventure. Don't let
getting older drag you down (who knows how long
it will take you to get back up again), embrace your
fabulous forties and let life begin!

# YOU KNOW YOU ARE 40 WHEN...

- You need to sleep in a bed - your mates' sofas are no longer acceptable pass out zones

- No amount of caffeine or fried food cures your hangover

- You crave tidiness and order

- You'd rather stay in

- You don't 'get' Snapchat

- You've switched from Radio 1 to Radio 2

- Spontaneity is a thing of the past

- Your social circle has become smaller, but better

- Home décor becomes a hobby

# COLD CUCUMBERS WILL DO NOTHING FOR YOUR PUFFY EYES

# THERE COMES A TIME WHEN YOU HAVE TO STOP CROSSING OCEANS FOR PEOPLE WHO WOULDN'T EVEN JUMP PUDDLES FOR YOU.

UNKNOWN

# A WORD FROM THE WISE

At the age of 20, we don't care what the world thinks of us; at 30, we worry about what it is thinking of us; at 40, we discover that it wasn't thinking of us at all.
Unknown

Stop whining about getting old. It's a privilege.
Amy Poehler

To get back my youth I would do anything in the world, except take exercise, get up early, or be respectable.
Oscar Wilde

It takes courage to grow up and be who you really are.
E.E. Cummings

Age is whatever you think it is. You are as old as you think you are.
Muhammad Ali

# 80s & 90s TRIVIA
## (PART 1)

1. Which song spent the longest as UK number one during the 90s?

2. South Africa's new prime minister in 1989 started to dismantle apartheid, what was his name?

3. In 1987, which song played at Scott and Charlene's wedding in Neighbours?

4. In what year did the Bank of England £1 note stop being legal tender?

5. Who challenged Margaret Thatcher for the leadership of the Conservative Party in 1990, resulting in her resignation?

6. Which film popularised Ray-Ban Aviator sunglasses?

7. Who in 1986 became the youngest ever Heavyweight boxing champion of the World?

8. What are the six colours on a standard Rubik's cube?

9. Who was Nirvana frontman Kurt Cobain married to?

10. Which supermodel first coined the phrase: 'We don't wake up for less than $10,000 a day'?

(See page 94 for answers)

# THINGS TO DO NOW YOU'RE 40

- Go on your dream holiday
- Support a cause
- Research your family tree
- Dress to impress...yourself
- Invent your signature dish
- Wear sunscreen every day
- Flirt with confidence now you're truly comfortable in your own skin
- Eat at a 3-star Michelin restaurant
- Have the best sex of your life

# TRAIN FOR A MARATHON... OR A 5K RUN AT LEAST

# WHY DID THE BIRTHDAY CAKE GO TO THE DOCTOR?

# BECAUSE IT WAS FEELING CRUMBY!

# YOU'RE HAVING A LAUGH

Forty is the age when, even if you have a great build, your stomach decides on a career of its own.

Children despise their parents until the age of forty, when they suddenly become just like them — thus preserving the system.
Quentin Crewe

Know how to prevent sagging? Just eat till the wrinkles fill out.

Let's drink some Red, Red Wine because UB40

I'm 40 but I still feel like I'm 20...then I hang out with some 20-year-olds and think 'nope, never mind, I'm 40'.

MY AFTER FORTY FACE FELT FAR MORE COMFORTABLE THAN ANYTHING I LIVED WITH PREVIOUSLY. SELF-CONFIDENCE WAS A POWERFUL BEAUTY POTION.

NANCY COLLINS

# A WORD FROM THE WISE

You only live once, but if you do it right, once is enough.
**Mae West**

Sometimes we're all too quick to count down the days that we forget to make the days count.
**Unknown**

The first forty years of life give us the text: the next thirty supply the commentary.
**Arthur Schopenhauer**

All we have to decide is what to do with the time that is given us.
**J.R.R. Tolkien**

You don't stop laughing when you grow old, you grow old when you stop laughing.
**George Bernard Shaw**

# DID YOU KNOW?

The two greatest environmental causes of excess wrinkles are exposure to sunlight and cigarette smoking. So stub out the ciggies and plaster on the sunblock!

As you get older, your teeth become less sensitive. This is because over time more dentin – the hard inner tissue – is built up between the outer enamel of a tooth and its central nerve.

Older women may have sex less frequently than their younger counterparts...but it's better. Perhaps it's the shedding of inhibitions or knowing what you want, but in studies of women 40 and over, researchers found that sexual satisfaction improved with age.

# THE MOLECULE RESVERATROL, FOUND IN WINE, CAN SLOW THE AGEING PROCESS...

**However, before you get too excited, there's not enough of it in wine to make a difference.**

# 40 THINGS YOU SHOULD KNOW BY THE TIME YOU TURN 40 (PART 1)

- How to live in the moment
- Never look in a mirror under strip fluorescent lighting
- Hard work gets results, not luck
- How to keep a secret
- A good read is a wonderful thing
- Obsessing over the past is pointless
- Nothing beats a good night's sleep
- Tinfoil can't go in the microwave
- De-cluttering is good for your health

# HITTING THE SNOOZE BUTTON IS NEVER A GOOD IDEA

# YOU'RE NEVER TOO OLD

Rudyard Kipling won the Nobel Prize in Literature when he was 41.

At the age of 44, George Washington crossed the Delaware River and captured Trenton, New Jersey.

Samuel L. Jackson had only ever played bit parts before landing an award-winning role at 43 in the Spike Lee film Jungle Fever.

At 42, Madame Tussaud opened her wax museum.

AGE 40, VERA WANG DECIDED THAT SHE WANTED TO BE A DESIGNER. SHE COMMISSIONED HER OWN WEDDING DRESS FOR $10,000 AND OPENED HER FIRST BRIDAL BOUTIQUE THE FOLLOWING YEAR.

# YOU KNOW YOU ARE 40 WHEN...

- You don't get the slang these days
- Bedtime is something you really look forward to
- You're no longer embarrassed to complain in a restaurant
- If the milk smells strange you don't drink it
- Dinner parties with your friends involve meals cooked from scratch
- You still have a CD collection
- You take more photos of people than 'cool stuff'
- You get over-excited if someone IDs you
- You take responsibility for your own happiness

# THE CHILD YOU USED TO BABYSIT IS NOW YOUR DOCTOR

# TOO MANY PEOPLE MISS THE SILVER LINING BECAUSE THEY'RE EXPECTING GOLD.

## MAURICE SETTER

# A WORD FROM THE WISE

There are far, far better things ahead than any we leave behind.
C.S. Lewis

When I passed forty I dropped pretence, 'cause men like women who got some sense.
Maya Angelou

Learn from yesterday, live for today, hope for tomorrow.
Albert Einstein

We don't understand life any better at forty than at twenty, but we know it and admit it.
Jules Renard

We have to be able to grow up. Our wrinkles are our medals of the passage of life. They are what we have been through and who we want to be.
Lauren Hutton

# 80s & 90s TRIVIA
## (PART 2)

1. In 1992, who said 'I'm not sitting here as some little woman standing by my man like Tammy Wynette' following her husband's infidelity?

2. Who became the first woman inducted into the Rock and Roll Hall of Fame in 1987?

3. In 1990, who became the youngest ever Snooker World Champion in UK history?

4. Spitting Image spent three weeks at number one in 1986, but what did they stick up their nose?

5. In which year was Nelson Mandela released from prison?

6. Who designed pop star Madonna's provocative corsetry?

7. Which 1990 movie was directed by Martin Scorsese and starred Robert De Niro, Ray Liotta and Joe Pesci?

8. What was the name of the ferry that capsized off Zeebrugge in 1987?

9. What position did Douglas Hurd hold in 1989?

10. Who gained international recognition for her New Romantics clothes designs?

(See page 95 for answers)

# THINGS TO DO NOW YOU'RE 40

- Re-evaluate your life and alter your direction as necessary
- Avoid the drama
- Quit that bad habit
- Apply for your dream job
- Master the art of delegation
- Read the classics
- Climb a mountain
- Grow something edible
- Go on a road trip

# MASTER A CLASSIC COCKTAIL

# THE BEST PART ABOUT BEING 40 IS THAT WE DID MOST OF OUR REALLY STUPID STUFF BEFORE THE INTERNET.

# YOU'RE HAVING A LAUGH

When you hit 40, multitasking means you can sneeze and pee at the same time.

Congratulations! You have now reached the age where all compliments will be followed by 'for your age'.

When your friends begin to flatter you on how young you look, it's a sure sign you're getting old.
Mark Twain

Time wounds all heels.
Dorothy Parker

The best years of a woman's life - the ten years between 39 and 40.

# 40 THINGS YOU SHOULD KNOW BY THE TIME YOU TURN 40 (PART 2)

- Not everybody has to like you

- You need to exercise

- Who you are and what you want

- Shots are never a good idea

- Not to sweat the small stuff

- Your days of shopping in Topshop are over

- Don't judge people – you have no idea what journey they are on

- Teeth don't make good bottle openers

- Where your talents lie

# IT'S BETTER TO BE A RADIATOR THAN A DRAIN

# BLOWING OUT SOMEONE ELSE'S CANDLES DOESN'T MAKE YOURS SHINE ANY BRIGHTER.

UNKNOWN

# A WORD FROM THE WISE

At twenty years of age the will reigns; at thirty, the wit; and at forty, the judgment.
**Benjamin Franklin**

The great thing about getting older is that you don't lose all the other ages you've been.
**Madeleine L'Engle**

Forty is when you actually begin even deserving to be on stage telling people what you think.
**Jerry Seinfeld**

If life really begins on your 40th birthday, it's because that's when women finally get it... the guts to take back their lives.
**Laura Randolph**

Don't waste your time looking back, you're not going that way.
**Ragnar Lothbrok**

CHARLES THURBER PATENTED A TYPEWRITER AGED 40.

# YOU'RE NEVER TOO OLD

At 40, Mother Teresa left behind everything she knew and established the 'Missionaries of Charity', which eventually became a worldwide organization and led to her receiving the Nobel Peace Prize at the age of 69.

Singer Susan Boyle was 48 when she was discovered on TV talent show Britain's Got Talent with her rendition of 'I Dreamed A Dream' from Les Miserables and became an international star.

George Foreman recaptured the heavyweight boxing championship at the age of 44, proving age is no barrier to fitness.

Aged 43, music teacher William Herschel discovered Uranus.

# YOU KNOW YOU ARE 40 WHEN...

- Saturday night is just another day of the week

- You have no clue what's on MTV

- Most days you choose comfort over style

- Clubs with sticky dance floors hold no appeal

- You've made a mixtape in the past

- The only new celebrities you recognise are the offspring of the ones you grew up with

- You've found your first grey hair/s

- Plastic pint glasses are not acceptable drinking vessels

- You can remember life before the Internet

# YOU OWN
# SLIPPERS

# A WORD FROM THE WISE

As we grow up we realise it is less important to have lots of friends, and more important to have real ones.
**Unknown**

Act as young as you feel. You're not getting older, you're getting more entitled to be your fabulous self.
**Gwen Stefani**

The only time you really live fully is from 30 to 60. The young are slaves to dreams; the old servants of regrets. Only the middle-aged have all their five senses in the keeping of their wits.
**Hervey Allen**

Be on the alert to recognise your prime at whatever time of your life it may occur.
**Muriel Spark**

In the end it's not going to matter how many breaths you took, but how many moments took your breath away.
**Shing Xiong**

# THERE'S NEVER ENOUGH TIME TO DO ALL THE NOTHING YOU WANT.

## BILL WATTERSON

# THINGS TO DO NOW YOU'RE 40

- Confront bullies
- Ask each of your friends to teach you one new thing
- Learn a craft...and make something
- Host parties at home
- Write a poem
- Learn to foxtrot
- Try one more time
- Stay at home on New Year's Eve
- Stop being a slave to fashion

# VOLUNTEER IN A SOUP KITCHEN

# FORTY ISN'T OLD...
# IF YOU'RE A TREE.

# YOU'RE HAVING A LAUGH

Life begins at 40... but so do fallen arches, rheumatism, faulty eyesight and the tendency to tell a story to the same person, three or four times.
**Helen Rowland**

She said she was approaching forty, and I couldn't help wondering from what direction.
**Bob Hope**

My seven-year-old daughter walked in while I was getting ready for work. "What are you doing?" she asked.
"Putting on my wrinkle cream," I answered.
"Oh," she said, walking away. "I thought they were natural."

When you're 40, you still have all the moves – you just don't make them as fast.
**Melanie White**

Old enough to know better, but young enough to do it anyway.

# DID YOU KNOW?

A happy marriage could save your life...or at least prolong it. People in happy marriages tend to live longer. It's worth noting that getting rid of a troublesome spouse can also improve your longevity!

After the age of 40 many of us will need reading glasses, as we struggle to focus on objects up close, due to the hardening of the surface of the eye's lens.

We now know, thanks to more sophisticated brain scanning methods and technologies, that we hit our cognitive peak between the ages of 40 and 68. Over the years, our brains build up connections and recognise patterns, making us more effective problem-solvers and able to more quickly grasp the gist of an argument.

THERE WERE 1,578 BABIES BORN TO MOTHERS AGED 45 AND OVER IN ENGLAND IN 2009, IN 2015 THERE WERE 2,119. THAT NUMBER CONTINUES TO RISE TODAY.

# 40 THINGS YOU SHOULD KNOW BY THE TIME YOU TURN 40 (PART 3)

- Frittering your time away on people you don't much care for is not an option

- It's ok to say you're too busy to do something

- Being kind is always the best option

- Your body is beautiful

- Everyone is just trying to make their own way in life

- Fringes are your friend

- There is such a thing as too much stuff

- Worrying is pointless

- You are responsible for your failures

# A SOAK IN THE BATH MAKES EVERYTHING A LITTLE BETTER

# EUGENE ATGET, NOW CONSIDERED ONE OF THE GREATEST EVER PHOTOGRAPHERS, TOOK UP PHOTOGRAPHY AT THE AGE OF 40.

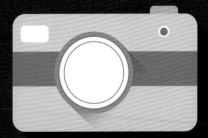

# YOU'RE NEVER TOO OLD

At 44, Sam Walton opened the first Wal-Mart and became one of the richest men in the world.

Tim and Nina Zagat had each turned 42 before they gave up their legal careers to write their first restaurant guides, now internationally acclaimed as the gold standard in restaurant reviews.

Aged 46, Alfred Eisenstaedt captured what became an iconic moment in history when he took his famous photo of a sailor sweeping up a girl in a kiss during a V-J day celebration in Times Square.

Stan Lee created the legendary Marvel Universe throughout his 40s.

# YOU KNOW YOU ARE 40 WHEN...

- You think going to IKEA is a valid weekend day trip

- All your favourite bands are performing reunion concerts

- You realise your mum was right after all

- You know who you are

- Everything you think happened 5 years ago actually happened 10, maybe 15, years ago

- It's just too hard to party all night

- You're no longer addressed as 'Mademoiselle' in France

- Skin care is now a thing

- You've started belittling the latest fashion trends

# YOU PAY FOR A TAXI INSTEAD OF GETTING THE NIGHT BUS

# 80s & 90s TRIVIA
## (PART 3)

1. Name the Wham! member who went on to record a multiplatinum record in 1987.

2. Which building in London opened its doors to the public in 1993?

3. Which girl group had number one hits in the 80s with 'Walk Like An Egyptian' and 'Eternal Flame'?

4. In E.T. the Extra-Terrestrial, what was the name of the boy who found the alien?

5. The 1985 Live Aid concert was organised to assist victims of what?

6. In 1994, 61 million people were still using what form of outmoded technology?

7. What was the name of Madonna's first album?

8. Who became the first child actor to be paid a million dollars for a film?

9. In what year was the search engine Google founded?

10. Who sang the 'Friends' theme song?

(See page 95 for answers)

# SO MANY BOOKS, SO LITTLE TIME.

## FRANK ZAPPA

# A WORD FROM THE WISE

We are all visitors to this place. We are just passing through. Our purpose here is to observe, to learn, to grow, to love...and then we return home.
**Australian Aboriginal proverb**

I felt like at 40 I had the right to say and be who I wanted to be, say what I wanted to say, and accept what I didn't want to accept.
**Halle Berry**

Laughter is timeless. Imagination has no age. And dreams are forever.
**Walt Disney**

In three words I can sum up everything I have learned about life:
It goes on.
**Robert Frost**

If you live to be a hundred, I want to live to be a hundred minus one day so I never have to live without you.
**Winne the Pooh**

# THINGS TO DO NOW YOU'RE 40

- Go on a night out to the opera

- Buy a piece of art

- Learn another language

- Try a new sport

- Drop that toxic friend

- Ditch drastic diets

- Pay your bills on time

- Go on a solo holiday

- Take your parents out to dinner

# LEARN TO PLAY A MUSICAL INSTRUMENT

# NOW THAT I'M 40 I TAKE LIFE WITH A PINCH OF SALT. PLUS A SLICE OF LEMON AND A SHOT OF TEQUILA...

# YOU'RE HAVING A LAUGH

I need more friends who understand that I still want to be invited but I'm not going.

After forty a woman has to choose between losing her figure or her face. My advice is to keep your face, and stay sitting down.
Barbara Cartland

They are not grey hairs, they are my wisdom highlights!

Pete: Do you like the dictionary I bought you for your 40th birthday?
Steve: Sure. It's a great present but I just can't find the words to thank you enough.

It's never too late to be what you want to be...unless you want to be younger, then you're screwed.

# THE BAD NEWS IS TIME FLIES. THE GOOD NEWS IS YOU'RE THE PILOT.

## MICHAEL ALTSHULER

# A WORD FROM THE WISE

Life really does begin at forty. Up until then, you are just doing research.
**Carl G. Jung**

Don't just count your years, make your years count.
**Ernest Meyers**

If we could be twice young and twice old we could correct all our mistakes.
**Unknown**

As time goes on, you'll understand. What lasts, lasts; what doesn't, doesn't. Time solves most things. And what time can't solve, you have to solve yourself.
**Haruki Murakami**

Everyone is the age of their heart.
**Guatemalan Proverb**

# DRINKING SODA CAN PREMATURELY AGE YOU. HARVARD RESEARCHERS DETERMINED THAT PHOSPHATE FOUND IN FIZZY DRINKS CAUSED MICE TO DIE EARLIER THAN PHOSPHATE-FREE RODENTS.

# DID YOU KNOW?

We get grey hairs because our melanin reserves, the pigment that gives our hair its colour, become exhausted at some point. When exactly this happens differs from person to person, with both genetics and stress playing a major role.

Muscle mass in both men and women begins to decline as early as in one's 30s, replaced by ...wait for it...flab.

You most definitely care less about what people think of you. Research on peer influence shows that our desire to fit in with others begins to plummet after young adulthood, with doing what you perceive is right being your prime motivation rather than what you think will meet other people's expectations. Go you!

# 40 THINGS YOU SHOULD KNOW BY THE TIME YOU TURN 40 (PART 4)

- A smile goes a long way

- What other people think of you is none of your business

- You make your own reality

- Nobody is perfect

- Who your true friends are

- Quality not quantity

- You can't change people, only your reaction to them

- To trust your instincts

- How to be yourself

# YOU CAN NO LONGER EAT CAKE, PIZZA, CHIPS, BISCUITS... AT THE RATE YOU ONCE DID

CHARLES BABBAGE WAS IN HIS 40S WHEN HE PROPOSED A LARGE-SCALE DIGITAL CALCULATOR, THE 'ANALYTICAL ENGINE', THUS CREATING THE CONCEPT OF A DIGITAL PROGRAMMABLE COMPUTER.

# YOU'RE NEVER TOO OLD

Soviet cosmonaut Georgy Timofeyevich Beregovoi joined the cosmonaut corps aged 43.

Harriet Beecher Stowe published her antislavery novel **Uncle Tom's Cabin** when she was 41.

At 47, Edward Jenner, an English doctor, pioneered the use of vaccination against smallpox.

At 43, Annie Taylor, a widowed schoolteacher, went over the 160-foot-high Horseshoe Falls in a barrel.

# YOU KNOW YOU ARE 40 WHEN...

- You relate more to the parents than the kids in TV shows

- You have more standard photos than selfies in your camera reel

- You don't take photos just because they're Instagramable

- Your hangovers last for days

- Your tolerance for reality TV stars is rapidly declining

- You don't care what other people think of you

- You hate noisy pubs

- You can't quite believe that people were born in the 2000s

# YOU ONCE LISTENED TO CASSETTE TAPES...

# ...AND RECORDED YOUR FAVOURITE SONGS FROM THE RADIO

# LIFE IS A BOOK AND YOUR FORTIES ARE THE CHAPTERS WHEN IT ALL STARTS MAKING SENSE.

UNKNOWN

# A WORD FROM THE WISE

And the beauty of a woman, with passing years only grows!
**Audrey Hepburn**

Your age is measured by your dreams not by the years.
**Amit Ray**

Youth. I don't seek it through another because I have it within; it's a state of mind, a spirit that is free, and a mind that is playful.
**Donna Lynn Hope**

When you love what you have, you have everything you need.
**Unknown**

Age is opportunity no less than youth itself.
**Henry Wadsworth**

Be wise with speed; a fool at forty is a fool indeed.
**Edward Young**

EXERCISE CAN REVERSE MANY
AGE-RELATED CHANGES WE MAY
START NOTICING OVER THE AGE OF
40. EVEN JUST A DAILY WALK CAN
REDUCE BLOOD PRESSURE, HEART
RATE, INCREASE LUNG CAPACITY AND
STRENGTHEN THE IMMUNE SYSTEM.

# DID YOU KNOW?

Studies have shown that you're more empathetic in your 40s than during any other decade. This ability to tune into how others think and feel can be incredibly beneficial to all your relationships, from loved ones to colleagues.

The average time we spend eating is 67 minutes a day, so over a lifetime we'll spend on average about 3.66 years, or 32,083 hours, of our life noshing. Yum.

Skin wrinkles because we start to produce less and less collagen – which gives skin that youthful, plump lustre – from around the age of 20. After a number of years of depleting collagen levels, skin becomes fragile, thinner and more susceptible to the ravages of gravity.

# THINGS TO DO NOW YOU'RE 40

- Give more compliments

- Take a stand

- Take part in an adrenaline-filled activity

- Make amends

- Donate a percentage of your earnings to a chosen charity

- Make some new friends

- Start saving for retirement

- Drink good quality wine

- Discover your superpower

# SCHEDULE A HEALTH CHECK-UP

# AGE AND GLASSES OF WINE SHOULD NEVER BE COUNTED.

# YOU'RE HAVING A LAUGH

Middle age is having a choice between two temptations and choosing the one that'll get you home earlier.
**Dan Bennett**

The 'I just woke up' face of your 30s is the 'all day long' face of your 40s.
**Libby Reid**

There is only one cure for grey hair. It was invented by a Frenchman. It is called the guillotine.
**P.G. Wodehouse**

Age is like the newest version of a software. It has a bunch of great new features but you lost all the cool features the original version had.
**Carrie Latet**

The best thing about getting older? Knowing someone is an arsehole before they even speak.

# ABOVE ALL, NEVER LET AGE EXTINGUISH THE FIRE OF YOUR INNER CHILD.

## S. AJNA

# A WORD FROM THE WISE

The other day a man asked me what I thought was the best time of life. 'Why,' I answered without a thought, 'now'.
**David Grayson**

A fortieth birthday is like standing on a precipice - it's like seeing what you got in life and what you chose to give a miss. It is that obscure feeling of belonging nowhere - sometimes you are here, sometimes you are there. But this disorientation is meant to be enjoyed thoroughly - it will finally lead up to your beautiful destiny.
**Unknown**

Live as if you were to die tomorrow, learn as if you were to live forever.
**Mahatma Gandhi**

Wrinkles should merely indicate where the smiles have been.
**Mark Twain**

# YOU'RE NEVER TOO OLD

Umberto Eco wrote his first novel, The Name of the Rose, at 48.

Julia Child published her book, Mastering the Art of French Cooking, when she was 49, launching her career as a celebrity chef.

Henry Ford was 45 when he created the revolutionary Model T car.

Alan Rickman, who played Snape in the Harry Potter films, didn't land his first film role until he was 41.

# AT 40, PHYSICIST WILLIAM STURGEON CREATED THE FIRST ELECTROMAGNET.

# YOU KNOW YOU ARE 40 WHEN...

- You used to head for the mosh pit...now you need allocated seating

- You can hold a conversation about variable rate mortgages

- You won't buy a bottle of wine that's under £6

- You actually own spare bedding and towels for guests

- Fashionable youngsters in their twenties are wearing what you wore when you were ten...

- ...and you refer to people in their twenties as 'youngsters'

- The pop anthems of your youth feature on 'retro' playlists

- More of your friends are getting divorced than engaged

- You dye your hair to cover the grey, not for fun

# YOU USE THE EXPRESSION 'I'M GASPING FOR A CUP OF TEA!'

# THINGS TO DO NOW YOU'RE 40

- Be happy for other people rather than jealous

- Wave goodbye to obligation

- Don't look back

- Take a yoga class

- Start a new exercise regime

- Edit your possessions

- Meditate

- Have a heart-to-heart with your parents

- Spend more time with your family

# GET A GOOD HAIRCUT

# 80s & 90s TRIVIA
## (PART 4)

1.  Which album released in 1982 became the best-selling album of all time?

2.  What year did soap opera Eastenders first appear on British TV screens?

3.  Who won the men's final at Wimbledon in 1993?

4.  Which actress starred in the classic 80s films The Breakfast Club and Pretty In Pink?

5.  In a speech to Guildhall, Queen Elizabeth referred to which year as her 'Annus horribilis'?

6.  Who uttered the immortal words 'Oh Mickey you're so fine, you're so fine you blow my mind, hey Mickey!'?

7.  Which popular band were uncovered as a hoax in 1990, when their manager was forced to admit that they had been miming to tracks recorded by other singers all along?

8. 'With or Without You' appeared on which U2 album?

9. Which 90s TV show featured characters Tommy, Zack, Kimberly, Billy and Trini?

10. In 1986, the United Kingdom and France announced plans to construct what?

(See page 96 for answers)

# YOU'RE NEVER TOO OLD

At the age of 43, Lee Ermey's infamous performance as Gunnery Sergeant Hartman in Full Metal Jacket was his first major acting role.

At 46, a Scottish surgeon, James Baird, discovered hypnosis.

Great Britain's Jo Pavey won the European 10,000m at the age of 40.

John Glenn became the first American to orbit the Earth at the age of 40.

AT 46, RICHARD ADAMS WROTE **WATERSHIP DOWN**, ONE OF THE BESTSELLING CHILDREN'S BOOKS OF ALL TIME, SELLING TENS OF MILLIONS OF COPIES AND CAUSING FLOODS OF TEARS UP AND DOWN THE COUNTRY.

# IT'S OFTEN ONLY AS BEAUTY FADES THAT IT BECOMES APPARENT IT WAS EVER THERE.

## JANE TARA

# A WORD FROM THE WISE

If you're 40 years old and you've never had a failure, you've been deprived.
**Gloria Swanson**

Ageing is not lost youth but a new stage of opportunity and strength.
**Betty Friedan**

Youth has no age.
**Pablo Picasso**

The tragedy of life is not death but what we let die inside of us while we live.
**Norman Cousins**

Ageing reminds you of your ungratefulness of yesterday.
**Ben Tolosa**

# ANSWERS: 80s & 90s TRIVIA

## (PART 1)

1. 'Everything I do (I Do It for You)' by Bryan Adams

2. F.W. de Klerk

3. 'Suddenly' by Angry Anderson

4. 1988

5. Michael Heseltine

6. Top Gun

7. Mike Tyson

8. Red, Blue, White, Yellow, Green and Orange.

9. Courtney Love

10. Linda Evangelista

# (PART 2)

1. Hillary Clinton
2. Aretha Franklin
3. Stephen Hendry
4. A deckchair
5. 1990
6. Jean Paul Gaultier
7. Goodfellas
8. The Herald of Free Enterprise
9. Foreign Secretary
10. Vivian Westwood

# (PART 3)

1. George Michael, with Faith
2. Buckingham Palace
3. The Bangles
4. Elliot
5. Famine in Ethiopia

6. Pagers
7. Madonna
8. Macaulay Culkin
9. 1996
10. The Rembrants

# (PART 4)

1. Thriller by Michael Jackson
2. 1985
3. Pete Sampras
4. Molly Ringwald
5. 1992
6. Toni Basil
7. Milli Vanilli
8. The Joshua Tree
9. The Mighty Morphin Power Rangers
10. A tunnel under The Channel